Angels, Aliens, and Crazy Mom

Real reality is not so bad.

Janet Johnson

ISBN: 9798386229856

CONTENTS

FORWARD

A memorial serves as a tribute to the person, and in Jamie's honor, I will speak the truth. Throughout my life, I was instructed to stay silent, but I am breaking this pattern and "pulling a Jamie" by being honest. Jamie acknowledged the chaos of the world we live in and provided comfort to many by being a sympathetic listener who believed in their words.

The rest of us Johnson girls, apart from Jamie, labored to conceal the truth about our home life. Seeking help often worsened the situation, and the unwritten rule was to pretend as though everything was fine. However, as adults, our perspectives have changed. I am now speaking out for various reasons, including encouraging others living in dysfunctional households to know that they can still thrive in the long run. My sisters and I turned out alright, capable of seizing opportunities, handling most challenges, and circumnavigating toxic individuals to achieve our goals.

Numerous factors prevented most of us from disclosing our dysfunctional upbringing. During our time, it was customary to keep quiet about one's problems, and only the most dysfunctional and out-of-control families were identified. Teachers and other educators assumed that children from these toxic backgrounds would struggle academically and need remediation instead of rigorous coursework. I have been in many meetings where my colleagues told me that students from dysfunctional homes could only benefit from support instead of academic challenges, not realizing that many students were thriving despite their adverse circumstances. My sisters and I concealed our family situation from the schools because it was embarrassing, unlikely to be believed, and could reflect negatively on us.

One of the unintended advantages of hiding our dysfunctional background was that we were not placed in classes or services meant for "at-risk" kids. Now that the topic is not taboo, many successful adults have shared their experiences growing up in toxic environments with one unloving, uncaring, manipulative parent. They learned how to navigate the situation and succeed, with some saying their experiences made them better people. Teachers and school counselors must realize that if a student is succeeding academically despite living in an "at-risk" situation, they need challenging and rigorous educational opportunities, and can succeed without support from their families. When I taught eighth-grade math, I often questioned why highly achieving seventh-grade students were placed in remedial math classes. The answer was always that they had an unfavorable home situation and would, therefore, not have the necessary parental support to succeed in standard or advanced courses. This thinking still dominates education, but we must acknowledge that children from dysfunctional backgrounds can succeed academically and in life with the right support and opportunities.

1. CRAZY MOM

I don't ever remember a time when Mom wasn't crazy. I have a very good memory. I remember when they brought Julie home from the hospital. I was two. Jamie, Jennifer, and I sat on the couch, and each got to hold her—kind of. I also remember thinking that grownups think kids don't think or feel or take in what is going on around them, and that when I grew up, I was going to remember that they do.

Growing up, we only gradually became aware that our situation was not normal. Outside the house, and in front of other people, Mom would act completely normal, intelligent, capable, and even fun. People would tell us how wonderful she was. She acted crazy in front of Dad, but it was as if he could do nothing about it, so he never talked to us about it. Our Dad had no power in the family. He was nice and supportive to us kids. He played games with us. He taught us to play chess and never let us win. He would judge our drawings and tell each one of us that ours was the best, but not to tell our sisters. Mom only did things with us where she had an adult leadership role, where she could enjoy doing things and get recognized. She had no interest in what we did. One of the strangest parts of our childhood was that other people would tell us how wonderful, capable, and talented our mother was. The contrast between what we knew and what people said would have made us think we were crazy if we kids didn't validate reality for each other. Mom acted like a wonderful person to our teachers, people at church, our friends, and eventually to our spouses. We only talked about how crazy Mom was to each other and a few close friends in the neighborhood. Thank goodness there was no social media back then for her to create an electronic scrapbook showing what a wonderful mother she was. She had to build that persona by doing things like being in a high position in the local Girl Scouts, making the church bulletin boards, and acting normal in public. She could neglect us while doing those things (which was a blessing to us). Boy, if she had had social media, we would have had to participate in events with her to provide regular wonderful mom photo opportunities. This would have made the strangeness even more pronounced and would have required us to act as if things were wonderful for the photos.

At age two, I knew Mom was crazy. Jamie was four. We shared a room and from the time I could talk, we'd review the crazy things Mom did when we went to bed. We spent all the years that we lived at home navigating around her and trying to figure out what was wrong with her. We picked up early on that we were not supposed to talk about how crazy mom was, and that we were to pretend as if nothing ever happened when she would have raging tantrums or do something crazy. Jamie and I could talk openly in our room at night.

Our closest neighborhood friends knew Mom was crazy because eventually they witnessed her rages and general behavior toward us when she was not playing to an audience. Some of the neighbor kids' parents did not allow them to go in our house. No one ever said why, but we assumed it was because they knew our house was dangerous. There was little air conditioning then for people of our social status, and most of the neighborhood windows were open all summer.

This was all we knew growing up. For about the first ten years of life, I thought we kids caused her to act crazy because she regularly told us how worthless, lazy, and good for nothing we were—that she hated us and that we had ruined her life. She usually said these things calmly, but occasionally she would say them as she ramped into a rage. I don't remember ever being hurt by her saying those things. We were always reading the situation and trying to figure out if we were about to be in danger. When she talked like that, I would just try to figure out what kind of mood that meant she was in, and what might be coming next. She would have tantrums, maybe beat one of us during her tantrum, or destroy the house by throwing and breaking things.

So, what are we calling crazy? There were many dimensions to this craziness—so many that, now, as senior citizens, when my sisters and I describe a difficult co-worker or client to each other, we can refer to one of Mom's patterned behaviors. Mom's behavior was very patterned, and we studied those patterns to be able to navigate around her. We learned to recognize those patterns in other people. We might be describing someone and say, "You know when Mom would act like some simple thing was really complicated and as if she were being victimized by being expected to use some tool—like a sponge on a soap holder, for example? This person has that same way of acting difficult and crazy in a deniable way." Or, "You know Mom's food allergies that spring up out of nowhere and change all the time, to control whoever is fixing the holiday meal? Well, this person does that same thing anytime we go to lunch at work." We have all worked with or known people who have sometimes only one of Mom's crazy patterned attributes. Mom's craziness had many dimensions. Her craziness included violent rages and child-like tantrums. She also made up lies about family members or her history to illustrate how she was victimized and to vilify people. She would tell these stories matter-of-factly and was good at it. They sounded believable and true. As we grew older, she started having diet needs that were always changing and we had to comply with whatever food disorder or diet need she claimed at the time. Not only did she have food allergies, but she could claim to have illnesses that she had never had symptoms of because she either ate or didn't eat certain foods. For example, she claimed to have goiter but had never been diagnosed for it, nor had any symptoms, because of her diet. She'd say that if we used certain ingredients in meals, we would cause whatever diseases she currently didn't have to suddenly show up.

She would also routinely, purposefully leave things behind, like her purse in a restaurant, or clothes in a hotel so that we'd have to go back and get what she left and not be able to do what we had planned. We all learned to watch her for this. The only way to avoid the inconvenience she was trying to create would be to secretly pick up whatever she left and pull it out when she announced that we had to go back for it. She came to North Carolina from Illinois to visit when my son was a toddler. When I took her to the airport to leave, it was pre-911 and I could go into the gate with her. She left an expensive scarf she had been wearing in a bathroom out in the main part of the airport. I saw her take it off and lay it down, so I picked it up when she wasn't looking. When we got to her gate, she exclaimed that she left her scarf in the bathroom and it was her favorite one and we had to go back for it. Doing so would have caused her to miss her flight. Of course, I had the scarf. Her missing the flight would have been my problem to solve, so she would have enjoyed that. Or alternatively, it would have been my fault that she lost her favorite expensive scarf, and I would have had to buy her a new one. She rarely left items when there wasn't a huge consequence for recovering them. For example, she left her purse in a restaurant halfway to St. Louis when we were going to a ball game from mid-central Illinois. She remembered it and we had to go back about an hour's drive to get it. If there was not going to be a huge consequence, we learned to leave whatever she left. If you spoiled her fun of causing a huge inconvenience, you'd pay some other way.

Her tantrums were kind of spooky. Sometimes she didn't yell or scream during them. It was as if she were in a trance. A lot of her tantrums occurred when she got up from a nap. She took naps every day. We'd hear that bedroom door open and hold our breath to see what was going to happen. Sometimes she'd just come down, sit in her chair in the living room and light up a cigarette. She chain-smoked Camel non-filters, and she drank black coffee from sunup to sundown. She had a huge, event-sized coffee pot on the kitchen counter, and a big ashtray with water in the bottom of it. She kept water in the bottom of the ashtray because it got so full that the cigarette butts in there would otherwise catch on fire. Some days, she would have one of us bring her a cup of coffee while she lit a cigarette, and everything would be fine. Other times, she'd just quietly come downstairs and instead of sitting down, she'd walk over to the table in the dining room where we kids kept our homework and she'd rip it all up and throw the pieces around, or open cupboard doors and start throwing dishes, or take one of us kids and start beating us. But, if the doorbell or phone rang, she could come out of this instantly and be normal, cheerful, and completely coherent. Dad was not home when these tantrums occurred. I am not sure how much of her behavior Dad was aware of. It was absolutely taboo to talk about.

The riskiest time was when she woke up from her nap. Most of the violent fits happened then. One day, Mom woke up from a nap while I was cleaning the kitchen. I was on my knees scrubbing under the sink. Mom was in one of her fit trances. She calmly walked into the kitchen and started throwing the coffee cups that hung under a shelf. Then she walked over to me and grabbed me by the hair and started banging my head against the pipe under the sink. I was trapped and couldn't get away. Jamie and Julie were there. They got her off me.

She once threw the dishes out of the cupboards, toppled furniture, ripped up papers, then took a box of Oxydol powered laundry soap and poured it over the mess. The Oxydol on everything made cleanup much harder. After other tantrums, we'd comment that at least there wasn't Oxydol on everything as we cleaned up. After a tantrum, she would go upstairs in her room and we kids would clean up her mess. We always cleaned them up while she went upstairs and waited for us to remove any sign of her tantrum. She then acted as if they never happened. This was very strange. If we did not have each other to talk with about what happened, we would have felt crazy going from the rage, chaos, and destruction to acting as if nothing had happened and everything was fine. There was no gradual transition. It was like an on-off switch. Jamie and I used to wonder to each other what would happen if we ever failed to clean up after a tantrum. We were too afraid to try it. And for Jamie to be afraid is something.

When Dad was working the night shift at one of the local factories, she would wake us up in the middle of the night by turning the radio up full blast, turning on all the lights, running the vacuum sweeper in our bedrooms, and get us up to do some crazy chores. She'd be in a sort of trance-like anger state. Jennifer and Julie were awakened in the middle of the night along with us to "learn to make sandwiches" or to clean the house. Dad took salami sandwiches on white bread with yellow mustard to work in his lunch. Everything Mom did was organized, orderly, and usually way more complicated than it needed to be. This night, we had all been asleep for hours when she turned on all the lights and the radio full blast. She had us go downstairs and stand at the counter while she laid out the bread to make six or so sandwiches and threw the salami like Frisbees at us. We always made a week's worth of Dad's lunches at the beginning of the week and froze them. Maybe one of us made them wrong or something. Dad would never have complained. We did not know what triggered these events—if anything did.

If she destroyed our homework, we just had to work around that. We were all very good students and a few missing homework assignments wouldn't hurt us much. We were supposed to put our homework on a specific spot on our buffet at night. If something was really important or a long-term project, I would either not bring it home or would hide it. She once ripped up Julie's Dick, Jane and Sally book. Because of the unwritten but very real rule that we were not to talk about what Mom did, we couldn't explain missing work. We'd have to make up a lie.

Julie was in first grade. She didn't know what was going to happen when she didn't have her reading book. She got to school the next day and the teacher handed her a new book and said that Mom had called and explained what happened. We always wondered what explanation Mom gave. It is doubtful that she explained that she was having a tantrum and tore it up. We suspect she may have blamed it on Julie. In junior high school, I had a Latin project with a partner. We researched the Greek and Roman gods and made a poster describing and comparing them. We spent weeks on this. I had it home the night before it was due. I had to finish some things to turn it in the next day. It was too big to hide, and Mom knew I had it, so I put it on the buffet and tried to act as if I didn't really care about it. It was too much for her. She could see how much work had gone into it, so she had a fit and ripped it up. A very good friend of mine was my partner. We were both getting high As in Latin. I think we still got As. I told her that Mom ripped it up. That was one of the first times I told anyone about Mom, outside the neighborhood. This friend said it was okay and we just took the 0 and did not make an explanation for why we had no project to turn in.

Sometimes, Mom would be busy with a project, like sewing or planning a Girl Scout or family camping trip and she'd be enjoying what she was doing and just totally ignore us kids. During those times, if I could keep her from needing to cook or clean or take care of anything, she would

stay happy because she was focused on something she really enjoyed.

Now, as a 66-year-old adult, I think that I could keep her happy by

making sure she had no work to do when she was engaged in something

she enjoyed. But, as a child, I thought I could keep her from having what

we called "fits" at any time, by making sure she had no work to do ever.

I still watch people around me who seem to get upset if they must work,

and I try to do the work for them without being noticed to keep them

from acting unpleasant. I would far prefer to do additional work than to

be around a negative or toxic person who is acting out.

2. BUILDING REALITY

As young children, we learn to interpret reality based on our experiences. My sisters and I grew up in this household, where we were not only learning to navigate around our mom, but strangely, everyone who thought she was wonderful, talented, and intelligent. The world at home was completely different than outside the house. My favorite book as a child was the Lion, the Witch, and the Wardrobe because my world was like theirs in the book. My homelife was chaotic and violent, and I had to be super aware, but step out the door and the world was calm, and everyone was nice, and my Mom was a different person. She smiled, was friendly and treated us kids nicely. It was like going through the door into another world. Jamie and I would talk at night and try to figure out reality. How old were we? I can't say, because we talked every night about this as far back as I can remember. In addition to our crazy mom and discussing how to survive every day, we discussed religion.

We did not know what was real and what wasn't real. We sure could see that all the adults we knew pretended to live in a reality very different from ours—that our Mom was wonderful, talented, and great to be around.

When we started school, we went to L. T. Stone Elementary School in Galesburg, Illinois. Mrs. Gotcheff was our principal. She was also a Sunday School teacher at our Christian Science church. I don't know why we were Christian Scientists. None of Mom's family was. I think it was a virtue signal or "special signal" thing for Mom. Dad never went to church with us. He didn't own a suit and said that was why he could not go with us. Christian Scientists don't believe in doctors or traditional healthcare. But, we went to the doctor. All of us kids were vaccinated, but for camp and school when we were supposed to provide proof of vaccinations, Mom would instead provide a card saying that because we were Christian Scientists, we did not need to provide this. She implied that we were not vaccinated, yet we were.

There were two Sunday School classes in the basement of the First Church of Christ Scientists in Galesburg. The little kids: Tina, Laurie, and our sisters Jennifer, and Julie, were in one and the big kids: John, Linda, and Jamie, and I were in the other. We mostly had to memorize verses of the Bible and would be instructed about how, if you think correctly, you will never have any illnesses. Like Mom's fits and the dysfunction in our house, no one ever talked to us about the things we learned at church that might not make any sense. The fact that our elementary school principal was one of two Sunday School teachers in our church made me think that what I was learning at church was equivalent to what I was learning in school. I thought I had to learn what they were teaching, just like I had to learn to read and do math.

Christian Science teaches that illness is imagined, and members are not supposed to go the doctor. Jamie and I would discuss at night how all the old people in the church wore glasses. This made no sense to us since they were teaching us that if we think correctly, we will never have anything physical wrong with us. We would ask about these things at church and be given the signal not to ask questions like this.

One of the things that we memorized was a string of sentences in answer to "Who is God?" The answer was that he was "all knowing, all being, omnipresent, omnipotent supreme," etc. I thought we had to know and understand what we were learning, with the principal in charge and all. I did not know the words omnipresent nor omnipotent, so I asked what they meant. Mrs. Gotcheff explained that these mean he is everywhere and all powerful. I explained that to my sisters, so we'd better understand what we are being taught. Mighty Mouse was a cartoon we watched. To Julie, this meant that God must be like Mighty Mouse: "He's here, He's there, He's everywhere, So beware." So, she answered "Who is God?" with that Mighty Mouse song after I explained this to her. She was sent out of the classroom for punishment. This may be what started her "brat" streak, which she had from then on—and has to this day. Julie also answered, "John," when asked who God was. She thought that the only boy in Sunday School, John, must be God because she thought that God lived at church and was a boy. Once again, she had to sit out in the hall. In both cases, Julie wasn't trying to be onery. She thought these answers were correct, based on what she knew. Julie wasn't even in kindergarten yet. I watched the adults' reactions to her misunderstandings. I could see why these answers made sense to her. They acted as if she were misbehaving. That was curious to me.

We also had to memorize the commandments. I was probably in first grade, because John and I were the youngest kids in the big kids' class. Jamie and Linda were the older kids. Jamie would have been in third grade, and Linda in second. We all had to do the same work. In Christian Science churches, members cannot attend the church service until they are 18. Sunday school was a lot like school, only more confusing and boring sometimes. We had lessons, mostly memorizing

things, and we'd take turns showing that we had done so in class. Then

the teacher might tell us a story from the Bible. I had developed the need

to figure out what we are supposed to do and do it from trying to

navigate the world of Mom. I thought it was super important that we

never do the things that the commandments say not to do. This was

presented as the top ten list of things you can never do or should always

do, and we had to memorize the list. Do not kill, was easy to understand.

I tried to get some clarification as to whether this included insects. I

never really got any. But what the heck was committing adultery? How

am I going to not do it if I don't know what it is. So, I asked. My

elementary school principal, the highest authority that I knew, explained

that committing adultery meant mixing good with bad and gave the

example of mixing orange juice into milk and ruining both. My thought

was "Seriously?!That is as bad as killing?" Whatever. I was just trying

to make sense of reality. What did I know? It seemed to me that killing

would be so much worse than mixing orange juice into milk, but there is

so much about this reality that doesn't make sense to me that I am open

to anything.

Not long after getting clarification on what committing adultery meant,

we were having a birthday party in our yard on West North Street. The cousins and neighbors were there. Our next-door neighbor Jimmy was kind of a brat already, in a class clown sort of lovable way. He was funny, usually. For the party, we had root beer Fizzies. These were like Alka-Seltzer tablets with sugar and flavor in them for people who could not afford soft drinks. We had them at birthday parties. The kids all got a glass of water and a Fizzy tablet. Jimmy was watching his like a science experiment. The bubbles were fizzing up. He scooped up dirt and added it to the glass. We only got Fizzies on very special occasions. I could hardly believe that he ruined his Fizzy. I yelled to the adults, "Jimmy is committing adultery!" I thought he was breaking a commandment as bad as killing—although I didn't understand why it was as bad as killing, but a lot of reality didn't make sense to me. The adults all laughed. They didn't do anything. They were probably smoking and drinking beer. I tucked that aside. Jamie and I discussed this that night. Something is wrong with this religion thing. They make us memorize the list of the ten worst things you could ever do and then when Jimmy is doing this, they laugh. They tell us that God is here, there, and everywhere and when Julie likens him to Mighty Mouse, she must sit in the hall. He seemed a lot like Santa Clause to me, but I dared not say that out loud. I learned from Julie's lesson.

There were only certain stories we'd read from the Bible. One of the stories that we heard repeatedly in Sunday School was in Luke, where the angel appeared to the shepherds, and they were terrified. The angel told them not to be afraid. And then they weren't. This terrified me. First, I couldn't distinguish between what I was learning at school and at Sunday school as far as how these things differed. My elementary school principal was the teacher, and she was teaching me this story. It didn't seem like something that could happen, but then again, maybe it could. I thought if you pray, an angel might appear which didn't seem like it would be that much different than seeing a ghost. In fact, I didn't see how it was any different from seeing a ghost. Terrifying. And then how would it get you to suddenly not be afraid, except for hypnotizing you or taking control of your mind? There was no way I was going to pray. And I hoped none of my sisters would conjure one up, either. The only prayer we ever said in our house was before meals, "God is great. God is good. Let us thank him for our food. Amen." I didn't feel like that would risk conjuring up a ghost-like supernatural being who would take control of my mind and make me not be afraid of a terrifying event. That was a safe prayer.

We also learned at church that anything physically wrong with you, like an illness or even an itch or pain from sunburn, could be eliminated if you thought correctly. I wasn't quite sure what "correctly" meant. The

Science and Health with Key to the Scripture by Mary Baker Eddy was not very clarifying, either. (Later in life when I read Willa Cather's book on Mary Baker Eddy and Mark Twain's book on Christian Science, I understood why it wasn't clarifying.)

By the time I was six years old, I was constructing my understanding of reality to include trying to understand how life outside the home could be so different than life inside the home, how thinking correctly would heal any physical problem—and correct thinking should involve praying but that could conjure up a supernatural being. And no one else seemed concerned about these things. There were contradictions everywhere, like the emphasis both at home and church on washing our hands or covering your mouth when you cough. If germs couldn't make you sick, why would my Christian Scientist principal and Sunday school teacher be so focused on having kids wash their hands. To add to my confused reality construction, I saw a public service announcement on television that said all aliens had to report to register at the post office by January 1st. The PSA sounded totally real. What alien meant to me were the monsters on Lost in Space. Sometimes they were even invisible. They were almost always dangerous and evil. I found Mom in the kitchen and told her that I had seen this PSA and asked if her aliens were real. She said they are real and there are probably some aliens teaching at Knox College, up the road. She said she thought one of the chemistry professors was probably

an alien. That took the cake. This was worse than angels. Dad would

run errands on Saturdays, including going to the Post Office. He would

take turns taking one of us girls with him. I was not going anywhere

near that Post Office in January.

Even though we were Christian Scientists, we went to the doctor

sometimes, and other times we didn't. Mom didn't seem to believe what

they taught. She seemed to enjoy the attention of explaining why

schools and camps could not require us to prove that we were vaccinated.

We had those big scars on our arms like everyone our age from one of

those vaccinations. But no one ever called her on it. People don't notice

much. Jamie got rheumatic fever when she was about 12. This was one

time Mom decided not to go to a doctor. She hired a Christian Science

Practitioner to come to our house to heal Jamie. Jamie and I shared a

room. After a while, Jamie couldn't walk. A home-study teacher came

to our house and taught Jamie in our bedroom. Jamie couldn't get out of

bed. The Christian Science Practitioner would come about once a week

and pray, read passages, and try to help Jamie think correctly so she'd

get well. I think Jamie missed most of seventh grade. By this time,

Jamie and I had figured that religion was pretty much bunk, and I was no

longer afraid that praying would conjure up supernatural beings. Jamie and I would laugh and make fun of the Practitioner when she wasn't there. The Practitioner brought Jamie a plant one day and said that Jamie was just like this plant, and she would flourish and grow just like it. The plant died a few days later. Jamie and I laughed about that and wondered how the woman would talk her way out of that one. Finally, one of the few times that Dad ever stood up to Mom, he insisted that Jamie be taken to the doctor. The doctor put her on penicillin, and she got well pretty quickly. Jamie and I quit going to church then. We claimed freedom of religion and said we did not like that religion. Mom went along with it, and we didn't have to go any more.

3. NEW INFORMATION FOR REALITY

And up until about age 10, I thought that we triggered Mom into acting

crazy. She always claimed that we did. We thought that if we behaved a

certain way, or better anticipated what she wanted, we could keep her

from acting the way she did. I was constantly looking for patterns in

Mom's behavior to figure out how to keep her calm, and to protect

myself from her schemes. We were lucky to learn that we weren't

triggering her behavior. It gave a whole new perspective to our reality.

Shortly after Jamie recovered from rheumatic fever, Jamie and I saw

Mom setting us up for the fit that she was going to throw by placing

things out-of-place in the living room. She didn't know we were coming

down the stairs. The "things" included open safety pins on the couch, so

we referred to this as "the safety pin incident" from then on. We could

tell she was in what we called "one of her moods," and she didn't see us.

We stopped and watched. She was carefully placing things on chairs and the couch very calmly. When we came into the room, she started ramping up into a screaming throwing fit, complaining about us kids leaving these things out instead of putting them where they belonged and how dangerous these safety pins were. This was a turning point for us and made a huge difference in our understanding of reality and how to navigate it. Until then, we believed that if we behaved perfectly and tried to be better people, that she wouldn't have these violent rages or be so mean to us. She frequently told us how worthless we were and how hard it was to be burdened with raising such stupid, lazy kids who were so thoughtless that we did things wrong and made work for her. After we saw her setting us up and then blaming us during her tantrum, we knew it wasn't anything we did. She created the evidence that we were worthless so she could rage about it. We didn't quite know how to process that, but we knew we had better never forget that. We talked about that "safety-pin incident" as a turning point for the rest of our lives. This is when we learned that this was not about us.

After the safety-pin incident, we quit trying to figure out how we could change our behavior and instead started trying to figure out what was wrong with her. We started questioning everything then. We had already figured out that our religion made no sense. We were supposed to think that if we could think correctly, we would never be sick and bug bites wouldn't itch. And if we would act correctly, Mom would never be crazy and mean. Neither of these major things that influenced how we thought about ourselves turned out to be true. Jamie and I discussed these things at night. I think Jamie started seeing life as a Live Action Role Play (LARP) event. Civil War reenactment, and Renaissance Fairs are LARPs. People know they are play-acting, but really get into their roles. I think we both started seeing our life as a LARP. We just reacted to this differently.

Jamie grew up just choosing what to believe and then going all in for it, like LARP. Then she'd change to some other belief system or perspective on reality since it is made up anyway. She lived on a commune for a while, was straight, was a lesbian, was a fortune teller who could read palms, joined countless 12-step programs, and had illnesses that required service animals before that was even a trend. She was very creative. As a young adult, one of my sisters might ask me what Jamie is doing now. I could answer, "She's a Christian head of La Leche league, and planning protests where women are going to breastfeed in the pews this Sunday," or "She is a fortune teller, volunteering at a Gay Pride event to raise money by reading palms." Or maybe, "I think she has terminal cancer this week, and has a comfort dog with her at all times, but I'm not worried because last month she had some other terminal disease and it was over before I knew what it was."

After we had claimed our religious freedom and quit going to church, Jamie joined the First Christian Church, a more mainstream, Protestant church, and went by herself. This was the beginning of Jamie doing LARP. Christian Science does not baptize. Jamie decided to get baptized in this church and, for some reason, she decided that Julie should also be baptized. We're not sure of the ages, but Julie believes Jamie was about 14 or 15, which would make Julie 10 or 11. Here's how Julie tells the story.

"Jamie came up to me one day and told me she had scheduled me to be baptized at the First Christian Church. She told me the date and time and I, being about the most complacent person in the world, agreed. I didn't even ask any questions. Jamie wants me to get baptized, okay. I'll get baptized. On the day the baptism was to take place, and about five minutes before the time it was to take place, I was playing in another church yard with my friend Geraldine. We were trying to do headstands, when I remembered that it was the day I was to be baptized. I looked in the neighbor's window to see what time it was. I told Geri we needed to ride our bikes to the First Christian Church—about half a mile away. We rode our bikes and didn't even bother to use the kickstands. We just tossed 'em on the ground and entered the church. I remember going inside and seeing about eight other kids dressed to the nines. They were dressed as if they were going to be flower girls or ring bearers in some big, fancy wedding. Their parents and grandparents were there, too, and they were dressed to the nines. Geri and I were dressed like ragamuffins. I remember my shorts were cut-off denim pants with flowers all over them. Geri was dressed in cut-off red denim shorts and a red nylon ribbed shirt with the sleeves cut off. I remember some of the grownups asking me where my parents were. I said they didn't come. I doubt they even knew about it, but I didn't figure that was relevant. All the grownups were treating me as if I were some poor, little waif. Only years later did I figure out they felt sorry for me. Here I was on one of the most important days of my life, and my parents couldn't even bother to support me. Jamie didn't show, either, but that didn't even seem like a slight to me. I was too naïve or stupid to be embarrassed about my appearance or the fact that I had no adults supporting me. Or the fact that I really didn't know what a baptism was.

"They sent all the family and guests to the pews in the nave and gave white gowns to all of us who were to be baptized. I put the gown on, and it turned out to be the great equalizer. Now, all of us children looked equal in flowing white gowns. From the pulpit area, I saw Geri sitting on a pew in the back. This church had a little pool in the sanctuary where we were dunked completely. After each of us was baptized, we stood at the front of the pulpit, kind of on display. We were dripping wet. I noticed Geraldine was doing all she could to suppress laughter. When it was over, I asked her what was so funny. She said the white robes turned see-through when they were wet, and once again I was the ragamuffin waif in the dirty play clothes, while my fellow "believers" were in their Sunday-go-to-meetin' clothes again. As for beliefs, I had none. I was probably a nominal Christian at the time; if you asked me what religion I was, I'd have answered 'Christian,' but I never gave it much thought.

"When it was all over, we got fed. There was a table with treats on it. Geraldine and I took as much as we could hold and still ride back to the other church to continue our headstand practice."

Julie told me about this years later. I am sure our parents never knew. When we weren't in the house, Mom had no idea and no interest in what we were doing. We were so used to this that we would never have thought to tell Mom about Julie's baptism.

Jamie and I both became skeptical of everything and knew that just because everyone is acting as if things are a certain way does not mean they are that way. Rather than become a LARPer like Jamie, I learned to become invisible and hide in the background so as not to be noticed by crazy people like Mom. It didn't always work. They tend to notice me and they can tell that I can tell who they really are.

I have seen people who have tantrums and behave toward their families the way Mom did with us. The family members walk on eggshells trying to keep them happy. I have also worked with people who have tantrums like Mom's. From watching Mom all those years and learning to look for signs that a tantrum is coming, I've learned to predict this behavior in other people. I've had bosses, co-workers, and other people around me who I've thought "This person is going to blow up today," after seeing them. They act differently when they are on the path to a blow up. It is not that different than a hungry toddler. It is easy to predict that they are going to blow. A hungry two-year old may think that their meltdown is triggered by the fact that the graham cracker didn't break exactly on the line, and now they must eat a non-rectangular cracker. At that age, they think the trigger is outside of themselves. But adults can usually tell that the two-year old is about to have a meltdown if they don't get fed soon. And just like the hungry toddler, they blame their blow up on some event or person. It was going to happen anyway. They may think the trigger is outside of themselves, but it is like something is wrong with their

chemistry. I think Mom staged the safety pins because she needed to

blow up to relieve her pent-up anxiety. She couldn't just blow up for no

reason, so she'd make reasons. I've seen other people do this. When

kids don't understand that they do not cause their parents' tantrums, they

grow up thinking something is wrong with them. It is much healthier for

kids to understand that the parent has something wrong with them and

simply blames the child or others for their behavior. I have seen a very

clever kid who could tell that her parent was going to blow up soon

create what I call "controlled triggers" to give them something to blow

up about. I wasn't clever enough to do that as a child.

4. THINGS WERENT THAT BAD

As kids, we knew that some people felt sorry for us because we were poor. Somehow that was communicated to us. There was no basis for people feeling sorry for us. Being poor didn't make us unhappy. We wanted things we didn't have, but so did all kids. I couldn't wait until I was old enough to work and would then be able to afford a Playdough Fun Factory. But I didn't lose any sleep over not having one. We were fine being poor. Our whole neighborhood—and probably our whole elementary school—was about in the same income class. It really wasn't that bad. It was the 1960s.

As bad as things were at home, we just learned to expect it and navigate around Mom as best we could. It didn't keep us from enjoying any other part of our lives. When we were in elementary school, we were outside all day in the summers, and all evening and weekends during the school days. Our neighborhood had a stable population, and some houses that rented to people with kids who came and went. The stable population of kids, of which we belonged, ran the neighborhood. We were unsupervised. We'd have clubs in the summer. The oldest kids, Jamie, Sally, and Mary would be in charge. You had to pay dues to be in the clubs, and we'd use the dues to hold carnivals. We'd order the Jerry Lewis' Muscular Dystrophy Association (MDA) back yard carnival kits. We'd plan most of the summer for the carnivals. They would be like the carnivals we had at school. We sold tickets and made posters advertising the event, just like we did for the school carnivals. Some neighborhood kids would shoplift the prizes. They'd spend the first part of the summer on shoplifting trips downtown to get superballs, and other small prizes for the games. The bus that went downtown stopped in front of our house. We'd just get on the bus and go downtown. We'd go to the Bondi building, which was the tallest building downtown and home to dentists' and doctors' offices and small businesses. We'd ride the elevator up and down, jumping up when it went down so we could experience a moment of freefall. Some kids would run next door to Kiddie Corner and shoplift. Then we'd get back on the bus and ride home. These activities were planned by the Club. Looking back, it is kind of stunning that we were in elementary school when we did this, and no one ever knew where we were. We Johnson girls had to come home when Mom rang the bell that was mounted on our porch. Someone would stay in hearing range of the bell and ride a bike to find us if we were out of range and it rang. Because Mom slept for hours a day, it was usually unlikely that she'd be calling us home unexpectedly.

No one ever shoplifted at Nelsons. This was the five and dime in our neighborhood. Pearl Nelson always knew what we were up to. We'd sit at her counter and eat snow cones while planning. We spent all our allowance there on penny candy. She was the only adult who ever knew what we were doing.

We'd have scavenger hunts to get money. We'd spend a day making scavenger hunt lists, with common items on them. We'd cross out most of the common items, and then put coins with specific but not rare dates on the list. In 1965, we might put a 1964 dime on the list. We'd hit different parts of town and keep track of where we had been recently. We could get anywhere on our bikes. We'd split up with these lists and knock on doors and tell the person that we are almost done with our scavenger hunt and very close to winning. We'd have some rare, unusual things not crossed out, and the 1964 dime. People would be very excited to help us win and say they might have that 1964 dime.

And they would because it was last year's dime. We'd hit every house in the targeted neighborhood and keep track of where we had been when in the club records. We'd meet back up at the club area. We kept the lists in a cigar box. This is how we got money to ride the bus downtown. I am not sure what we did with the rest of the money since we shoplifted all the prizes and charged admission to our carnivals. We probably bought refreshments for ourselves to eat and drink during our club meetings. Our clubs would have executive officers. We'd vote for president, vice president, secretary, and treasurer each summer. We'd also name the clubs and vote on a list of names. We'd decide whether to allow the temporary renter kids to join. We always did. We needed them to play outfield when we played baseball. We didn't have enough kids for two teams. When we weren't having club meetings, we were playing baseball, hide-and-seek at night, cards or board games, bike riding, or swimming at the YMCA or in the lake. We lived outside. We'd run all over town in the sewer system. The boys would throw cherry bombs in to scare out the rats, and then we would run under streets and come up to different parts of town. This avoided the trains of Galesburg. Galesburg has railroad tracks everywhere and I think we counted over 60 trains one day. Pearl eventually told our parents we were running around town in the drainage sewers because she was worried it wasn't safe. That was the only thing that Pearl ever told our parents. We quit doing this because it was so unusual for Pearl to rat us out to our parents. We thought maybe she was right.

Not only did we have our outdoor life with our neighbors, but we had school. I guess our neighborhood was poor. We didn't know it because everyone was poor. We were all the same. The range of different incomes in Galesburg wasn't that large. I had never been in the home of a doctor or lawyer. I did know a few girls who had real Barbie dolls instead of the imitations we had. My cousins had a living room kids couldn't go into, and their house was nicer than ours, but not that much nicer. Both of our grandparents had color TVs. We thought they were rich because of that. And they ate in restaurants. We had never eaten in a restaurant, except with them. I assume, at our neighborhood school, everyone must have been poor. A few kids were living with single moms, which was rare in the early 1960s. We had pretty good teachers, for the most part. My sisters and I did very well in school. Our clothes were ironed (by me) and our hair was clean and brushed. I wondered why some kids in our school wore wrinkled clothes and were dirty. I think the teachers treated us well because we were clean and neat, and we were good students. We also pretended to not live in a dysfunctional, crazy household. School was a haven for us because we were treated with respect, high expectations, and given positive feedback. We all loved it there.

We had a few crazy teachers, but we knew how to navigate crazy. My sister, Julie, had a crazy third-grade teacher. This woman was over-the-top crazy. She did not teach the kids anything. She must have been talked to about this, so she went nuts one day and told the kids that because they had done no work to date, she was writing their assignments on the board, and they had to complete them by the next day. Then, she filled the chalk board with assignments. A year's worth of work was going to be due the next day. One of Julie's classmates, Christine, who had normal parents, started crying as she copied what the teacher wrote, thinking she was expected to complete all this work that night. Christine thought adults were authorities, and of sound mind. Julie explained to her that this is just an episode that will be completely forgotten as soon as it's over and everybody will pretend as if it never happened. And she was right. That teacher never came back. That was her last day. A new teacher came in and this event was never mentioned.

I only had two crazy teachers in elementary school. I considered that good. My other teachers were wonderful. Some kids had trouble navigating crazy. Not me. I've always had an antenna for who might also be living with crazy people because they can navigate crazy. I watched for this trait in my peers. As an adult, I looked for this in kids. I can also usually spot adults who know how to navigate crazy, and many of them explain to me that they grew up with a crazy parent. As bad as it is growing up, you do get some good life skills.

Once we were in Junior High, we just spent as much time away from home as possible. Mom had gone to work as a teacher, and she thought we were old enough to take care of ourselves. By Junior High we had to buy our own clothes, cook all the meals, and do all the housework. It was a relief to a large extent because she mostly just ignored us then. It was easier to steer clear of her. And when she was engaged in something that interested her, like teaching her classes, she would ignore us.

5. SPECIAL

After we quit trying to figure out how to heal ourselves by thinking correctly, and how to have Mom behave like a normal person by behaving better, we started trying to figure out what was wrong with Mom. Jamie and I would discuss the patterns we observed and try to figure out the kind of illness she had. It didn't seem like just a simple mean person. There was a crazy element to whatever was wrong. We wondered if she had some specific mental illness. But we didn't think a person should be able to switch a mental illness on and off as Mom could do. We noted characteristics of her personality so that maybe as we read about mental illnesses, we would be able to spot some that described her traits. One trait we noticed was that she seemed to think she was special, as if getting more than her share of everything was fair because she was worth more. If there were two kinds of people, special and lesser, then Mom thought she was the special kind and Dad and his family were the lesser kind. Mom would tell stories that illustrated how inferior Dad's family was. She did this sometimes in deniable ways. Story details would convey how people in Dad's family weren't very bright or had bad character as little asides to the main stories.

Being special seemed to play a role in Mom's crazy violent behavior. She resented having to do any work unless it was intellectually stimulating to her. It also seemed to let her off the hook for who she hurt, because she was special and only hurt lesser people like us kids and Dad.

Mom's family seemed to also think she was more special than her sisters. Mom had two sisters, who lived near us, and they acted as if Mom were smarter, more talented, and somehow better than them. Both of her sisters were talented, nice, caring people. They babysat us, hosted the holiday meals, made our birthday cakes, made us clothes and I don't think Mom did anything for them. I know that Mom was given a car and went to college, but her sisters didn't. They talked about this as if it were right because she was so deserving, and super intelligent. We had old home movies of Mom, her sisters, and our grandparents. My aunts were dressed in raggedy old play clothes in the movies, and Mom was dressed in nice dresses playing with them. Somehow, this idea of special came early.

In addition to the stories Mom would tell that would illustrate her superiority, and therefore, her entitlement to whatever she wanted, she would tell stories where she was a victim. One of the stories that Jamie and I heard repeatedly was that as a child, Mom was a carrier of scarlet fever, although she didn't have it. She said they had just moved to a new apartment building when this happened. Her name was Shirley Jean Landon, and she says she was called Shirley up until then. Because she was a carrier of scarlet fever, she had to be quarantined. She told us that grandma would put a tray of food outside her bedroom door and leave. Occasionally, the other kids would be gone, and she could go into the courtyard for a bit to get out of her room. She said this went on for about a year. Then, when she was no longer a carrier of scarlet fever, she could play with the kids in the apartment building. But, during the time that she was quarantined, another girl named Shirley had moved in, so they told her she now had to be called by her middle name, Jean. Jamie and I thought that maybe this event caused her family to treat her as if she were special from then on because they felt so bad for her.

When Jamie died in 2021, I was talking to my cousin about Jamie's life. I mentioned that Mom being crazy and violent played a role in how we turned out. My cousins didn't know our mom was crazy. I told my cousin that we thought this scarlet fever incident may have played a role in how Mom was then treated as special by her parents, and that being special seemed to play a big part in justifying her behavior to herself. My cousin had never heard this scarlet fever story, and asked her mother, Mom's sister, about it. My Aunt said this never happened. She had never heard the story. My Aunt was completely sane. She said there is no way any part of this story is true, and that Mom was always called Jean, from birth. This was a shock to me. Although I figured that Mom made up many of the stories that vilified my Dad's family, I had not considered that these victim stories about her childhood were fabricated. We did notice that one of the old home movies of a Christmas after Mom and Dad were married showed Mom setting the table in their apartment with China that had a wheat pattern on it. We had one serving platter with this pattern on it that we only used on holidays. Mom told us matter-of-factly many times that she had chosen this pattern for her wedding China but she only received this one platter as a wedding gift. She told us that nearly every time she used it. She had a complete set of this China in the old movie. She most likely broke it all during fits. We didn't know it was a lie until we saw the old movie, when we were adults. Someone in the family transferred old film to video and we saw this after Mom was dead. She probably never told us that story in front of anyone who would have known it was a lie. She may have thought she needed to explain to us why we had one nice platter and no other nice dishes.

I have an antenna for the personality traits that seemed to have played a role in Mom's cruelty. I have seen many people who somehow come to believe that they are special. It is not that uncommon for people to mature out of childhood having developed a belief that they are a special kind of person. Not that they are good at something, but just inherently special and worth more than most people. Our culture has conveyed specialness to various demographic groups. Within any demographic group, a person can have the idea that they are special. The people who have this idea about themselves seem to believe it.

Rather than do their share of work or contribute, special people think they should get credit just for being there. They think they are entitled to more than lesser people. Being popular in high school can cause this. So can being the child of a family that owns a business in a small town, where other than doctors and lawyers, most parents are blue collar. It is kind of like a caste system, but only based in part on family lineage. One family member can be special, while the others are not. No one else in

Mom's family was special.

People can grow up thinking they are special, and not be mean or crazy. There are many ways that the idea that some people are special and just worth more than others get conveyed. I think that is what Hitler was thinking. That seems to be an underlying theme in Ayn Rand books. Cultures with caste systems believe some people are inherently better. One school system that I was working with started requiring testing for placement in special classes for gifted children. A staff member told me that some parents from India told the school that their children did not need to be tested because they had papers showing that they were from the Brahman class. I knew a person from a little town in rural America who wrote a letter to the school board in Raleigh explaining that her family was some superior kind of gifted, and therefore her daughter should be admitted into a gifted curriculum. This was the same idea as the Brahman class, except what made her family special was that they owned a small business in a tiny town where everyone else was poor. I've met people who believe they are special because they earned some award in a school in a small mid-western rural town fifty years ago.

This idea of being special is all around. Some of the self-help books and self-improvement movements of the 70s were designed to help people feel like or be mistaken for a special person.

Whatever special was, Mom had it and we didn't. I wasn't sure what made a person special, but it seemed to be a concept that other people recognized. When we were young, a family moved into the house on the corner, right next to us. It was one of the nicest houses in the neighborhood. But the houses didn't differ that much. Both the mom and dad were teachers. She was an elementary school teacher, and he was a high school English teacher. They had three kids in the same age range as all the kids in the neighborhood that we played with. The father met with our dad and another neighbor and explained to them that they were only temporarily living in our neighborhood. They were going to save money and move to a better neighborhood. So, they did not want their kids to play with us because that might taint them and give them habits and ways of being that would make them unacceptable when they moved to a more expensive neighborhood. The kids, two boys and a girl, were not allowed to play with us. We felt sorry for them because they had no one to play with. Our dad and the neighbor told this story and laughed and laughed at this guy for telling them this. This neighbor had expected that we'd respect them for moving into the special class. This was more evidence to me that being special meant it was okay to be cruel. Mom never commented on this, but Dad thought it was hilarious.

(Looking back now, I can kind of understand why they maybe didn't want their kids playing with completely unsupervised kids who ran around town doing some of the things we did. But, they didn't give that reason. It was simply the habits of our social class that they didn't want their kids to pick up. As an educator, I've been to many professional development events for teachers that explained the differences in habits of low, middle, and high-income people. In these workshops, it is implied that the habits of low-income people keep them from being academically successful.

We kids made countless fun of the soon-to-be-special family. We invented a card game named after them. The game was kind of like Kings Reverse. Each special card action was named after someone in their family, as if their names were verbs. We thought of this as mocking them. They eventually moved out of the neighborhood and sold their house to a professional Black family. The father met once again with the neighborhood dads and asked if they would object to a Black family moving in. Our dads told the story laughing about how any family would be better than this one. At least the Black family wouldn't look down on us and prohibit their kids from playing with us. They had a daughter, and her parents allowed her to play in the neighborhood.

Special people can be dangerous. They don't do their share of work, and they are entitled to whatever they want. Although I never thought it caused Mom's craziness and violence, I think her belief that she was special allowed her to not care about how she hurt people. Whatever this specialness is, it gives people a shield to not let other people's feelings get in the way of what they want. They only have empathy with other special people. This is probably why it was okay for slave owners to mistreat their slaves. Remember in Huck Finn when Tom is surprised that Jim loved his daughter? He'd always been told slaves didn't have feelings for their family members so it was okay to separate them from their children.

I saw other examples of specialness while growing up. Jamie got a job working at the Herrington Home for Children in Galesburg. She cleaned and worked in the kitchen. This was an orphanage or group home for foster kids. She made friends with three siblings who were living there off and on. Their mother had problems, and Children and Family Services removed them from their home more than once to live there. The two sisters were good looking, academically successful, well-behaved kids. I didn't know their brother well. He couldn't live there when he became a teenager. The place closed on holidays, so they came to our family's holiday dinners at my aunt's house with Jamie. The girls also spent the night at our house many times. At one point, they were available to be adopted and were by a Knox College professor and his wife. They adopted only the two girls. They were probably about 12 and 14 years old. This couple told them that they could no longer spend time with us because they were going to have a better life now. We were supposed to understand this, just like with our neighbor. They would sneak out and spend time with us anyway, but we had to hide it. Years later, I was attending Knox College and took a course from the professor who had adopted them. He did not remember ever having met me before, and I didn't remind him. As a Knox College student, he treated me as if I were one of the special kind of people. I took a physics class from him. He was a good professor and very kind and supportive to students, including me. I could tell that he assumed I was one of the special kind of people because I was attending Knox College, and I was good at math and physics. He tried to talk me into changing my major from math to physics. Previously, he had assumed I was not one of the special kinds of people because of where I lived, and because my sister, Jamie, cleaned for the Herrington Home. No special person would have a job like that as a teenager. He seemed to automatically assume that I was special when I was in his physics course at Knox. I have experienced this at other times, like when I had a Ph.D. with a minor in statistics and was analyzing data for a school system's research department. Many times in meetings, I would suggest that we should identify the high scoring low-income students for some challenging programs and others would explain to me how obviously I came from a high-income professional family and therefore would not be expected to know that low-income students would suffer if put in rigorous courses for reasons I was not expected to understand. I did not let on that I was not from the background they assumed because I could see how they thought about people from my background. I'm old enough to retire now, so I don't need to keep it a secret any longer.

Because the idea of specialness seems to be so pervasive in our culture, even though it is not discussed, it can take years if ever to understand that this is simply a manipulative technique that unbalances the idea of fairness. Instead of self-help workshops designed to teach people to feel like they are special and to convince others of the same, we should have workshops designed to reveal what nonsense and poison the idea of specialness is. Maybe Implicit Bias training should focus more on eradicating the myth that some people are more special than others. We should eliminate "gifted" from schools. No one who is in a special category wants to give it up. They don't want to hear that they are not really special. A lot of math teachers don't want to believe that almost anyone can learn rigorous math. Many of them believe you must be born

with a special gift of the ability to learn math and be a special kind of

person. This is not true. I know because I am not special and math is

very easy for me, and as a teacher I could teach math to nearly anyone,

regardless of how non-special they were. People seem to love the idea of

being special. I hate special.

6. TRYING TO GET HELP

Jamie may have had a right to be especially angry at Mom. She lay in bed unable to walk for months because Mom needed to appear to be a Christian Scientist. Mom never talked about religion or any of the beliefs from church with us. There was no praying, or any kind of religious discussion. It was like our schoolwork. It was just up to us to do our work and figure things out. So, it seemed kind of arbitrary that Jamie would lie in bed for months with rheumatic fever and not see a doctor. Mom went to the doctor when she was sick. Unlike me, Jamie didn't just observe, learn, and try to navigate our situation. She sometimes stood up to Mom. That just brought on more hostility. She also tried to get help. Dad had started working two jobs. He worked at one factory, Gale Products, on the first shift, then went next door to Admirals and worked the second shift. Mom always complained about how poor we were and blamed this on Dad not making enough money and us kids costing too much. Not only would working two jobs get him some peace to be out of the house and away from her, but maybe the additional money would make her happier. This meant he was gone from 7 a.m. until 1 or 2 a.m. He had given Mom ultimatums before to stop beating us kids. She stopped in front of him. But now that he was not home, she got worse. There was nothing to stop her. She had been waking us up in the middle of the night to clean, destroying our schoolwork, and she beat me unconscious once. I would never cry, which was so frustrating to her. So, if I got beat, it kept coming. She'd quit if you were crying and screaming. I just wouldn't give her that. I would just let her beat me.

Jamie wrote a letter in a spiral notebook to Dad telling him how bad things had become. Our neighbor, Sally, was Jamie's best friend. Sally knew how bad Mom was. Jamie passed this notebook to Sally to read during English class at Churchill Junior High. The teacher saw it being passed and took it. After reading it, the teacher gave the letter to the school counselor, Mrs. Jordan. Mrs. Jordan read the letter and called Jamie into the office. By this time, Mom had gone to work as a teacher. She was well known and respected. Mrs. Jordan was going to call Mom to come in and talk about what Jamie wrote. Jamie begged her not to and got her to call Grandma Landon, Mom's mother, instead. Grandma

Landon came and read the letter. Grandma took Jamie home, and like everything else, the incident was never discussed. But suddenly, Jamie had to start going to therapy. Jamie was furious. She went to therapy at Research Hospital once a week. Jamie never said a word while in therapy. She'd come home and tell me about it at night. She was so angry with this outcome. The teacher, Grandma, and the school counselor had read Jamie's description of what our home life was like, and no one did a thing except send Jamie to therapy. No one talked to us about it. They didn't even tell Jamie why she had to go to therapy. We wondered why Mom didn't have to go to therapy. We didn't know what happened to the letter. We didn't know if Dad saw it. We felt sorry for Dad because Mom was as mean to him as she was to us. She'd hit him and punch him as she did us kids. He just took it. We didn't see any way to stop her, so we didn't blame him for anything.

Jamie tried to get us help another time. Mom woke up from a nap and came downstairs in one of her trance-like states. She started having what we called a fit. During it, she picked up a bottle of salad dressing and threw it at Jamie. Jamie talked Julie into walking to the police station with her. It turned out the police captain's son was in Mom's science class. He sent someone to pick Mom up and bring her to the station. He explained to Julie and Jamie that they needed to respect their mother, and that kids are going to be punished and might think they are being abused. That was the end of that. Jamie gave up on getting help, and just started fighting back. Jamie got a job as a waitress and moved out into her own apartment while still in high school.

Years later, Jamie became a single Mom. Grandpa Landon had died. Grandma Landon moved in with Jamie to help with the baby. Jamie told me Grandma told her that she and Grandpa knew that Mom was nuts, evil, and violent, but they did not know what to do or how to help us. For Grandma to admit this meant so much to us. The hardest part of living in a family like this is the bizarreness of everyone acting like it is not happening. I can't imagine being an only child in a situation like this. We four kids had each other to validate our reality. My aunts and cousins claimed to have not known Mom was like this. They thought she was wonderful, talented, and great. I believe them, but it is hard to understand. Just having someone acknowledge that what we experienced was real is huge.

We kept trying to understand what was wrong with Mom. All of us four girls started reading True Crime books, especially where the killer appeared to be a normal person to everyone who knew them. One author, Ann Rule, worked with Ted Bundy and thought that he was normal. Her books are especially good for reading about people who appear to be normal to most, even though they are evil, manipulative, and basically nuts. I find it fascinating that people can miss so much that is right in front of them. So many people missed seeing Mom. It is interesting to me what people can miss. I wonder what I miss. I still learn to see things in people that I had been unaware of.

7. WHEN MOM WAS HAPPY

Mom always told us that if birth control had been invented, we would have never been born. She certainly did not want to be bothered with taking care of kids, doing housework, or cooking. We thought maybe the reason she was so crazy was because she only wanted to do what she wanted to do, and anything else made her have a tantrum. She never acted like a parent to us. She had no interest in what we did or where we were. She never knew what classes we took. She wanted as little to do with us as possible. I don't remember her ever asking me what I thought about anything. When we were in high school, she'd play charades, password, and other games she enjoyed because then it was like playing with adults. If she was happy and doing something that interested her, she was fine.

Mom was sociable. She was in card clubs, and a club of women that she called coffee club. When we were little, if a club met at our house, we had to stay upstairs and not make any noise. In the 1950s and 1960s, most clothes had to be ironed and the ironing board was always set up in our parents' bedroom. I noticed early on that having to do work made Mom very unhappy. My sisters and I still joke, for example, that if Mom cooked a meal someone was going to be wearing it. She couldn't get through cooking a meal without going into a fit and throwing the food, usually at one of us. And she hated ironing more than she hated cooking. So, I cooked, and I ironed. Mom was having coffee club one day in our living room. We kids were not allowed to go downstairs for any reason during coffee club. No exceptions. I was 5 years old. I had not gotten dressed yet and was ironing in my pajamas. The cotton pajamas I was wearing were very wrinkled and I thought they'd be beautiful if they were ironed. I pressed the hot iron to my stomach to iron the top. I got a very bad burn the shape of the iron on my stomach. Jamie and I tried to figure out what to do. The pain got worse as we put wet washcloths on it. We waited until coffee club was over before going down. Mom took me to the emergency room and they treated me. She didn't tell us that we did the wrong thing by not alerting her when it happened.

Mom liked to sew. She always had sewing projects. Her sewing stuff was always out. She kept the sewing machine always set up in the dining room. There was fabric and thread all over the living and dining rooms pretty much always. She would buy clothes that she didn't like, take them apart with her seam ripper, and then remake them. She'd change the collars or put a different kind of sleeve on them. She even bought shoes one time and took them apart and remade them. We didn't know if this was part of her craziness or if she would have done this even if she were not crazy. One project could take a month. The projects had many stages. She'd plan, make patterns with paper and maybe even make the new collar with paper before making it with fabric. She'd sometimes take two or three things apart and use the collar from one for another, etc. She was happy and left us alone when she was deep into one of these sewing projects. We liked to be left alone. Invisible was good.

She was also happy when she was camping. Like the sewing, getting ready for a camping trip was a huge project. We had to plan it by making lists. We then made all sorts of stuff to take, mostly things from the Girl Scout handbook. We'd make fire starters from bottle caps, wax, and yarn. We'd weave mats from newspapers to sit on. I am sure this was toxic, but we'd soak pinecones in different chemicals to add to the campfire for different color flames. First, we'd have to find and sort the pinecones. I hate lists and planning. Everything she did with us was so planned. Even though we kids cooked the meals, we had to write out the

menus and post them in the kitchen, and list all the ingredients.

8. THE STROKE

It seemed as if Mom always hated Dad. He just tried to keep her happy. None of us expected anything from her. After I had moved out, she told him she wanted a divorce. He left with nothing. She kept everything. He gladly walked away with nothing. I gave Dad my car so he could drive to work. It was a $100 car. I always had money. I was always working and saving. Mom and Dad always borrowed money from me. After Julie graduated and left, Mom lived alone for a while. Her house developed a crack in the chimney, which resulted in a carbon monoxide leak. She survived it, but had several strokes caused by the exposure. After recovering from the series of strokes, she had a hard time play acting like the wonderful person people thought she was. She started treating kids in her classes the way she treated us growing up. It may have been complicated by the fact that we kids were gone, Dad was gone, and she didn't have anyone to treat horribly and abuse, together with the lack of control from strokes, but whatever it was, she started being crazy at school. Growing up, we always heard what a wonderful teacher Mom was. Now we were hearing stories about her throwing things, dragging kids by their hair, and other familiar behavior. We just listened.

The school district did a "reduction in force," and got rid of some teachers. They could get rid of tenured teachers this way. Mom was on the list. She went to protest meetings and met another riffed teacher, and they ended up married. We could hardly believe she was getting remarried. Her husband had taught at the other Junior High in town, that we had not attended. I asked one of my friends who went to that school if she knew him. She did not know my Mom had just married him, and she answered with, "Oh my god, he was a horrible teacher. He taught us nothing, never graded our papers, and was so boring and mean." Then I told her that Mom had just married him, and she tried to back track.

When they had been married for several years, I was living in St. Charles, Illinois and going to graduate school. He called me one day and said that something was wrong with Mom. He said she was waking him up in the middle of the night, turning on all the lights and the radio full blast, and running the vacuum, and acting crazy. He then told other stories of her throwing tantrums and breaking things. I told him that this is what she does. He didn't think I understood. He went back to school and became a Certified Nurse Assistant and got a job at a nursing home. My sister, Jennifer, called me one night to tell me he was dead. My first thought was that she killed him. I had always thought that if any of us kids had been an only child that she would have killed us. Jennifer then explained that he had had a heart attack at work. I called Jamie and told her that he was dead and her first question to me was, "Did Mom kill him?"

9. LIFE IS GOOD

Jamie had moved out when she was in high school. I wanted to get out of high school and go to college. I got through high school taking random courses, mostly art. I wanted to enroll in college prep courses, but my school counselor wouldn't let me. She said I had to be more or less invited to take those courses, and that I was not college material. She instead enrolled me in a remedial English class in which I was one of a few in it who could read. We listened to records of books being read in this class. I thought of this situation as another obstacle that I had to get around. At the time, I wondered why other kids in similar situations actually believed their school counselors. As a professional, many other professionals who grew up in low-income families tell me they got the same treatment in high school, and mapped their way through higher education with no guidance.

I applied to a state school on my own with no help from school counselors or parents. I did not know about scholarships. I thought scholarships were for athletes or people who could play an instrument. I didn't apply for any. I would not have known how to borrow money. I don't think I even knew that was possible. I paid for this one semester, and then I had to quit because I was out of money.

I moved back to Galesburg. Mom was going to charge me more than I could afford to move back into my bedroom. Mom also told me that anything that I bought while living in her house belonged to her. So, she wanted to keep my stereo and a bookcase I bought at a yard sale. I did not want to live there, but I had no place to go at first. I quickly found places to sleep. I slept on Jamie's floor for a while and stayed with a few friends. I moved back to Charleston, where the state school I had gone to was, and got an apartment with my boyfriend, Duane. I got a job at KFC packing chicken in the backroom, while Duane pumped gas. He was in college still. I went to work at KFC one day and my co-workers were on strike. They were picketing in the parking lot. Growing up in Galesburg, a factory and railroad town, I had been raised to never cross a picket line. I just drove right by without stopping and got my first waitress job at a Wags in a mall. I learned that you could make a lot more money waitressing than you can working for minimum wage in a fast-food place.

I moved back to Galesburg after living with Duane's family for the summer. I moved up in the restaurant world, getting a job at a more expensive restaurant that served beer. I lied about my age to be able to serve beer, but no one checked anything back then. The tips were way better. I could live on this. When Duane's mother told me that I'd drag him down because I was a waitress and he was going to be a professional, I moved back to Galesburg. I didn't quite understand this idea of special, but I knew it was something that people believed in. My sister, Jennifer, got me a job at a coffee shop where she worked. Mom and Dad had gotten divorced. Julie had joined the Navy. Jamie was always doing something different.

Jennifer entered Knox College right after high school. On the last day of high school, her senior year, Jennifer was in the chemistry lab cleaning beakers and the teacher asked her where she was going to college. Jennifer told him she wasn't going to college. He wondered why not and was concerned about this. She told him she didn't have any money and had not even considered it. This teacher called the registrar at Knox College, whose daughter had recently died. His daughter was Jennifer's friend. She had died of a septic infection of some kind, unexpectedly.

Her parents had set up a scholarship in her name. It was past time to apply to college. This teacher was friends with the registrar and asked if Jennifer could have the scholarship that honored his daughter. They helped Jennifer enroll. Jennifer was going to Knox College when I returned home. She worked at the coffee shop for a while, then she became the midnight teller at the drive-through of a local bank while going to college.

I had learned that the better the restaurant, the more money you could make waiting tables. I was a very good waitress. I could handle crazy mean customers that seem to go out to eat for the joy of trying to make the restaurant staff miserable. I figure these folks are like Mom; when she'd feel the need to blow up and they need a trigger outside themselves. So, they go out to eat because surely the wait staff will provide a trigger. I've seen a lot of waitresses quit during a shift because they couldn't stand being treated so badly by crazy mean customers. They may complain that their drink has too much vermouth in it when it has none. I'd know this had nothing to do with the actual drink. So as not to upset the bartender, who just waived the bottle over the glass, I'd take it and put more ice in it, wait a minute, then take it back and ask them to taste it while I waited. This always worked. I'd take their steak that wasn't done right into the kitchen and turn it over and bring it back.

I only did this when I could tell the person just needs to be special and to vent their rage and there really is nothing wrong. I saw many waitresses take these things personally, argue with bartenders and cooks about redoing something that wasn't wrong to begin with and then get so stressed out by the double binds that they broke down and just walked out. Kids who figured out how to navigate crazy early on do well in dealing with the general public.

I got a job at a steakhouse where some members of the local golf club regularly ate lunch. These guys suggested that I go to work at the country club. They got me a job there. At the country club, the money was even better, and we got full benefits. One of my friends from high school, Peter, sometimes tended bar there for big parties. He was going to Knox College, where his dad was a professor. After setting up the party, and before it started, we sat chatting and Peter asked me why I was not in college. I told him I just can't afford it. He suggested that I might be able to get a scholarship from Knox. He brought me an application the next day and we filled it out. Peter took it in and submitted it for me. I was accepted to Knox with a full scholarship that was for a girl with high math ACT scores. It paid my full tuition. I kept working at the country club while going to school, so I could support myself.

Julie ended up being career Navy. She said being in the military was easy because they tell you what to do, and everything is fine if you do what they say. With Mom, the rules kept changing and you never knew what to do to keep out of trouble. After being enlisted for several years, the military put her through college and officers training. She became an officer.

Jennifer ended up working in banking. She got an MBA from the Kellogg School at Northwestern. She had a very successful career in banking compliance and risk management. I went into mathematics, statistics, and education. I ended up with a Ph.D. in math education. I started a small business that evaluates grant-funded programs. Jamie became a nurse and developed a specialization in nursing homes and geriatrics. She knew every law and policy related to Medicare, Medicaid, and elder care. She was a LARPer to the end.

We all so appreciate living in calm environments, and spending time with kind people. Some people might take these things for granted. After living like that for 18 years, you learn to enjoy and appreciate little things in life. One of the great benefits to growing up like this is perspective and the ability to observe, and to understand that things may not be as they seem. We also developed a sense of humor about the situation at a young age. We'd laugh about the predictable crazy stuff Mom would do. I've often wondered what people like her would think if they knew how predictable they were and that people laughed at their behavior.

I think the only way to help kids who are living in a dysfunctional home with a parent is to provide them with opportunities where they can thrive and acknowledge their situation. Don't tell them they must be misperceiving or lying because the parent in question is known to be a wonderful and special person. Help them develop the skills to get out when they are old enough to. If there is some other way, I don't know what it is. Confronting the parent has never had a good outcome in my experience. Whoever confronts the parent will be cut off from the kids. People have much more difficult lives than growing up in dysfunctional homes. If you are a kid in this situation, have a shared reality with someone who sees things as you are experiencing them is important. I hope that sharing some of my reality helps.